Inclusive Strategies for the Virtual Classroom

How to Build An Inclusive and Engaged Virtual Classroom

Copyright © 2020

All rights reserved.

DEDICATION

The author and publisher have provided this e-book to you for your personal use only. You may not make this e-book publicly available in any way. Copyright infringement is against the law. If you believe the copy of this e-book you are reading infringes on the author's copyright, please notify the publisher at: https://us.macmillan.com/piracy

Contents

How to create an inclusive online class 1
Creating Inclusive College Classrooms 6
Be Virtually Inclusive: Do's and Don't For Educators 33
Quick Ways to Be More Inclusive in a Virtual Classroom 50
Inclusive online teaching: 6 tips for the virtual classroom 59

How to create an inclusive online class

This includes our online classrooms. Here are some ways to use language to create diverse and inclusive classroom environments for all students.

P.S. These tips are good for traditional face-to-face classrooms as well!

Why is inclusivity important?

As educators, we strive to create learning environments where all students feel welcome and included as equal participants with their peers. Thus, the language we use should exhibit respect and sensitivity to all students, regardless of background, gender, culture, etc. Such considerations are particularly important in online education, where our students may come from a diverse population of intersecting identities.

Recognize and acknowledge your bias

Now, your first reaction might be, "I'm not biased." But the term "bias" just means how you see and relate to the world around you, and it's a product of your experiences, culture, and values. Most of us come to our classrooms from a typically Western experience and use Western names, examples, stories, etc. Think about how you present content and how your presentation might be viewed by someone with a completely different set of life experiences. Does that analogy comparing an American football play and a natural physical process necessarily translate for someone from another country who knows nothing about American football? I encourage you to spend some time before writing content, announcements, emails, essay questions, word problems, quiz questions, etc. thinking about how to be more inclusive.

Here are just a few examples of small changes that can make your classroom more inclusive:

Inclusive Strategies for the Virtual Classroom

Use universal phrases

When using American idioms, explain them. Not everyone in your class is an American and will understand typically American phrases.

Avoid binaries like black/white, male/female, gay/straight.

Use gender-neutral phrases

Use generic greetings like Dear students, Good Morning Folks, etc. when addressing the class in emails, announcements, video conferences, etc.

Do not assume someone's gender based on name alone. One way to clarify this is to introduce yourself using your pronouns (Hi! My name is Jennifer and I use she/her/hers pronouns). Ask students to share the name and pronouns they would like the class to use. Note that the singular pronoun "they" is an acceptable pronoun according to Merriam-Webster and the Penn State style manual.

When giving examples, be cognizant of being stereotypical about gender. For example, don't only use male pronouns/names when talking about a blacksmith or female pronouns/names when referring to a teacher.

Use inclusive examples/assessment

Look for ways to include or portray inclusion in your examples, assessments, written content, and images.

Use a variety of ethnic and gender-neutral names.

Include a variety of people in your examples and word problems. ie. include people who are differently abled, people from non-western culture, same-sex couples, etc.

Use a variety of current events or historical examples. Avoid using all Western examples.

Other word choices

Be aware of the words you use and how they might alienate, misrepresent, or offend some groups of people. For example, use:

significant other rather than wife/husband

differently abled rather than disabled

visually impaired rather than blind

winter break rather than Christmas break

people of color rather than minorities

etc.

Using inclusive language is more than "political correctness." Inclusivity is about respecting and celebrating people's differences and including those differences in their educational process. Studies show that increasing inclusivity eliminates unintentional barriers that may hamper a student's ability to relate to you and to the material, which in turn increases their engagement and learning.

Again, these are just a few examples to get you thinking about how your language can create an inclusive classroom environment.

Creating Inclusive College Classrooms

Inclusive classrooms are classrooms in which instructors and students work together to create and sustain an environment in which everyone feels safe, supported, and encouraged to express her or his views and concerns. In these classrooms, the content is explicitly viewed from the multiple perspectives and varied experiences of a range of groups. Content is presented in a manner that reduces all students' experiences of marginalization and, wherever possible, helps students understand that individuals'

experiences, values, and perspectives influence how they construct knowledge in any field or discipline. Instructors in inclusive classrooms use a variety of teaching methods in order to facilitate the academic achievement of all students. Inclusive classrooms are places in which thoughtfulness, mutual respect, and academic excellence are valued and promoted. When graduate student instructors (GSIs) are successful in creating inclusive classrooms, this makes great strides towards realizing the University of Michigan's commitment to teaching and to diversity and excellence in practice.

In an inclusive classroom, instructors attempt to be responsive to students on both an individual and a cultural level. Broadly speaking, the inclusiveness of a classroom will depend upon the kinds of interactions that occur between and among you and the students in the classroom. These interactions are influenced by:

the course content;

your prior assumptions and awareness of potential multicultural issues in classroom situations;

your planning of class sessions, including the ways students are grouped for learning;

your knowledge about the diverse backgrounds of your students; and

your decisions, comments, and behaviors during the process of teaching.

Each of these five aspects of teaching are addressed in this section. This information will assist you to teach in more inclusive ways. Much of the information in this section was drawn from focus group interviews conducted by CRLT in 1995-96 with female and male students from a variety of racial, ethnic, and religious backgrounds and departments or units. In these interviews, students identified multicultural issues related to classroom climate, course content and materials, and teaching methods. They also made recommendations about how classrooms could be made more inclusive. The examples used to illustrate particular issues in the sections that follow were taken from comments made by students during the focus group interviews and from the experiences of CRLT staff.

Choosing Course Content

Some GSIs have a great deal of control over the content of a course, especially the content of their section, while others do not. It is helpful for students to know the extent to which you, as a GSI, have control. If students criticize or make suggestions about course content, texts, material, etc., over which you do not have control, you should convey their comments to the faculty member in charge of the course and encourage them to do the same.

When you have some control over the content (including books, coursepacks, and other materials), the following two questions and their related suggestions should be considered:

Whose voices, perspectives, and scholarship are being represented?

Include multiple perspectives on each topic of the course rather than focusing solely on a single perspective. For example, if the topic is

Include, as much as possible, materials written or created by people of different backgrounds and/or perspectives. If all the authors or creators of materials in a course are male (or female), white (or another group), liberal (or conservative), etc., instructors will be sending a message about the voices that are valued and will be devaluing the scholarship of others who have written or created materials on the topic. (This guideline should be altered appropriately in courses where the focus of the course is to better understand a particular perspective or world view. Even these courses, however, should be attentive to the range of possible voices on a given topic.) On a related note, it is important to include works authored by members of the group that the class is discussing. For example, if the course deals with topics related to Muslims or Islam and the syllabus does not include materials written by Muslim authors, the message sent to students may be that you devalue the contributions of and scholarship produced by Muslims.

How are the perspectives and experiences of various groups being represented?

Include materials (readings, videotapes, etc.) that address underrepresented groups' experiences in ways that do not trivialize or marginalize these groups' experiences. Books that include a section on some aspect of diversity at the end of the text or books that highlight women, people of color, people with disabilities, gay men, lesbians, etc., in boxes and not in the body of the text can be seen as examples of the marginalization of these topics, groups, and group members' contributions. When it is important to use such books for other reasons, instructors have a responsibility to make students aware of the texts' limitations at the beginning of the course and to facilitate students' ability to read critically with these issues in mind.

Be aware of and responsive to the portrayal of certain groups in course content. For example, if an Asian country's policies are being used to contrast American policies, the policy of the Asian country should not always be used as a negative example (e.g., social policies in China) or always used as a positive example (e.g., business in Japan). You need to address the role of culture in foreign policies and not present policies as either wholly good or bad. Such treatment ignores the complexity of other cultures' policies or practices.

Increasing Awareness of Problematic Assumptions

An important early step in developing competencies to address multicultural issues in the classroom is to raise your awareness of issues that are multicultural and how they might manifest themselves in classrooms. In this process, it is useful to give consideration to assumptions that you may hold about the learning behaviors and capacities of your students. You may also hold assumptions that are tied to students' social identity characteristics (gender, race, ethnicity, disability, language, sexual orientation, etc.). These assumptions may manifest themselves in your interactions with students. You may need assistance in order to become aware of your assumptions. You should consider getting to know your students to be an ongoing process related to developing a positive classroom climate that promotes excellence.

Below are examples of assumptions, how they might be dealt with, and how you might learn more about your students through the process of addressing these types of assumptions.

Assumptions About Students' Learning Behaviors and Capacities

Assumption: Students will seek help when they are struggling with a class.

For a number of reasons, students do not always feel comfortable asking for help. In order to address this issue, you can request meetings with students as problems arise or make office hour meetings part of the course requirement (e.g., each student will meet with you after receiving his or her grade on the first assignment). The latter is an ideal method because it allows you the opportunity to meet one-on-one with every student. It also removes the stigma attached to going to office hours.

Assumption: Students from certain groups are not intellectual, are irresponsible, are satisfied with below average grades, lack ability, have high ability in particular subject areas, etc.

It is essential that instructors have high expectations for all students. For example, if a student earns a grade of C or lower, you should inform the student of the need for a meeting to discuss his or her performance. If students are absent, you should show concern about their absence when they return by asking if things are all right with them. If there are repeated absences, you should request a meeting with the student to discuss the situation. It is important for you to make initial contact with students; however, at some point, students need to take the initiative.

Assumption: Students from certain backgrounds (e.g., students from urban or rural areas, students who speak with an accent, students from specific racial or ethnic groups) are poor writers.

While the degree of writing preparation varies across the public school system in the US, students' regional background or group memberships do not serve as accurate predictors of the degree of preparation they received. Furthermore, you need to be sensitive to cultural differences in writing styles, recognizing that many standards apply to the evaluation of good writing. If a specific type of writing is expected for a given class, it may be useful to assign a short, ungraded assignment early in the term to identify students who may need additional assistance in meeting that particular writing standard.

Assumption: Poor writing suggests limited intellectual ability.

It is misleading to equate students' writing skills with their intellectual ability. Students have varying degrees of experience with "academic" writing. You have a responsibility to be explicit about what is expected and share with students examples of good writing done by other students. You should also alert students early on of their need to improve their writing and should suggest resources to them (e.g., Sweetland Writing Center consultations).

Assumption: Older students or students with physical disabilities are slower learners and require more attention from the instructor.

While there are many cultural assumptions about links between age or physical ability and one's intellectual capacity, these characteristics are not typically linked. Most classes do include some students who require extra attention from the instructor but such students cannot be readily identifiable by physical characteristics.

Assumption: Students whose cultural affiliation is tied to non-English speaking groups are not native English speakers or are bilingual.

If you feel that it is important to know whether students speak or understand other languages, you should ask this question of all students, not just those to whom you think the question applies. If there are concerns about students' academic writing skills, it would be best to meet with the students during office hours to discuss their work. One of the questions you could ask as part of your data gathering protocol is, "What were the languages spoken in the environment in which you were raised?" Following this question with appropriate probes would give you an opportunity to find out whether students are native speakers of English and, if not, how recently they became fluent. It is important to identify the source of students' difficulty with writing (or speaking), because identification of the factors that contribute to the problem will influence the actions taken to address the problem.

Assumption: Students who are affiliated with a particular group (gender, race, ethnic, etc.) are experts on issues related to that group and feel comfortable being seen as information sources to the rest of the class and the instructor who are not members of that group. AND/OR European American students do not have opinions about issues of race or ethnicity and members of other groups do have opinions about these issues.

One way to effectively deal with this set of assumptions is to pose questions about particular groups to the entire class rather than presuming that members of a certain group are the only ones who can reply. For example, questions could be phrased so that students would be able to share experiences of their friends or comments that they've heard as well as their own experiences. It would be best to let the class know that if any individual has experiences or information that she or he thinks would be beneficial to the class, she or he should inform you about such experiences or information. If you would like to hear from a particular student on a specific issue that relates to group membership, you should speak with the student privately instead of calling on the student when the issue arises in class. In this way, you can find out the students' ability to comment on the issue and willingness to do so publicly. This would avoid putting the student in an awkward position, particularly if the student lacks knowledge about questions related to his or her group.

Assumption: All students from a particular group share the same view on an issue, and their perspective will necessarily be different from the majority of the class who are not from that group.

You can regularly encourage all students to express different perspectives on issues, and you should not express surprise when people from the same "group" share opposing views or have a view consistent with the majority of the class. It is important to understand, however, that some students who are part of a "group" will feel hesitant to share views publicly that differ from the "anticipated group position" for fear of being admonished by members of their "group" or isolated from the "group" (e.g., an African American student expressing an anti-affirmative action view).

Assumption: In their reading, students will relate only to characters who resemble them.

This would most frequently occur in courses in which students read literature. Instructors should be careful not to treat with suspicion comments that suggest affiliation with a character that does not resemble the student in terms of race, ethnicity, gender, etc. For example, if a Caucasian student claims to feel her or his experiences resonate with an African American character, you should not dismiss her or his response, but probe for further explication about why she or he feels the connection.

Assumption: Students from certain groups are more likely to: be argumentative or conflictual during class discussions OR not participate in class discussions OR bring a more radical agenda to class discussions.

Participation levels vary across all students, with some students more comfortable in listening roles and others more comfortable taking the lead in class discussions. While these discussion styles may be influenced by students' past experiences, families of origin, and cultural reference points, a priori assumptions about student participation may hinder class discussion. It is important that you encourage participation among all students while also respecting the differences among students that will emerge. More equitable discussions can often be created by prefacing the discussion with a writing exercise that provides all students with the opportunity to clarify their thoughts on the discussion topic. It is also useful to remember that students' participation levels evolve over the course of a term as they become more comfortable with the course, their classmates, and the instructor.

Planning Considerations

There are a number of multicultural issues that should be taken into account during the planning process for any class. You need to become comfortable with your lack of knowledge about certain groups and seek ways to inform yourself (e.g., through experiences, readings, and/or conversations with faculty, peers, and students who are knowledgeable about the particular groups). Below you will find examples of the sorts of issues that might be considered in order to increase your awareness of multicultural issues during the planning process.

Accommodations

Students may have religious holidays and practices that require accommodations at certain times during the academic calendar year. Students with disabilities may also require special accommodations. To be sensitive to the religious needs of students, it is important to read the "Religious Holidays and the Academic Calendar" handout provided each year by the Provost's Office so that you are aware of the holidays that occur during the semester you are teaching. Contact Services for Students with Disabilities (763-3000) for information on ways that you can accommodate the needs of those students. At the beginning of the semester, ask your students to let you know if their attendance, their participation in class, or their ability to complete an assignment on time will be affected by their observance of religious holidays or practices, or because of a disability. Give advance consideration to requests for reasonable and fair accommodations. Some instructors ask for this information on data sheets that students complete on the first day of class.

Attendance

Students who are different in a highly visible way (women who wear Islamic clothing, African Americans or Asian Americans in a predominantly white class, students who use wheelchairs, etc.) can be penalized because of their visibility. In particular, absences of such students may be noticed more easily. For this reason, it is important to record all students' attendance at every class session (whether or not you use the information) rather than collecting a mental record of absences of highly visible students that may inadvertently and unfairly affect how you evaluate them.

Grading

When you use different criteria to evaluate the performance of students from certain groups, this can create tensions in the class because students tend to share their grades. Furthermore, if these criteria are applied based on assumptions you have made rather than on accurate information regarding the students, some students may be unfairly penalized. For example, having higher expectations for Asian American students in Asian language classes than for other students may unfairly penalize Asian American students who have never had any experience with the Asian language they are learning. With this in mind, you should ask all students about their prior experiences with the course content and should inform students of the criteria by which their performance will be assessed along with the rationale for differential evaluations if such a practice will be used.

Cultural Reference Points

Instructors who use examples drawn only from their own experience may fail to reach all students in the class. Given that examples are designed to clarify key points, you should collect examples from a variety of cultural reference points. For example, in 1995/1996 "Friends" was a sitcom that received high ratings. However, this show was less popular among many African American people than shows like "Living Single" and "Martin." Similarly, when using sports examples it is important for instructors to include sports in which women participate (e.g., track & field, figure skating, gymnastics, tennis, softball) as well as those in which male participants predominate (e.g., hockey, football, baseball). This concern can also be offset by asking about students' familiarity with an example before discussing it or asking students to produce examples of their own. You can also explain examples fully in order to reach a diverse classroom.

Instructional Strategies

Students bring an array of learning styles to a class. If you rely on a small repertoire of instructional strategies, you may provide effective instruction for only a small subset of your class. You should become aware of your preferred instructional strategies. For example, are sessions with small groups of students doing problem sets always conducted by asking questions? Are whole-group discussions preferred and the only method used? Once you have a sense of your strategy preferences, you should consider alternative techniques that will help your students learn more effectively. If you typically give mini-lectures to students, you might consider using visual materials (e.g., charts, diagrams, video), demonstrations, hands-on activities, cooperative group work, etc.

Controversial Topics

Class sessions that address controversial topics may result in any of the following unintended outcomes: (a) altercations between individual students or groups of students, (b) silence from students who feel intimidated or fear conflict, (c) the assertion and perpetuation of false stereotypes or problematic assumptions, or (d) the expression of offensive speech. There are no easy answers for dealing with these situations when they occur. It is best to work toward the prevention of these occurrences by investing time in the planning process. When working with a particular controversial topic, anticipate possible responses and how you might deal with differing yet passionate views on that topic. You should plan strategies that provide structure for these discussions and that foster students' ability to express their own ideas well while also increasing their ability to listen to and learn from others. In the interest of free speech, students should be encouraged to honestly share their views during discussions. Be prepared, however, to correct stereotypes and challenge students' assumptions when comments are shared. It can be a difficult task to reconcile the tension between challenging offensive speech and not suppressing free speech. You should also consider your own response to emotion in the classroom and use this awareness to inform the planning process.

Establishing agreed upon guidelines early in the class can be an important aspect of productive class discussions. If guidelines are established early, students will need to be reminded periodically of the rules throughout the semester, especially if their behavior suggests that they are ignoring them. If such rules were not established at the beginning of the semester, it is necessary to establish them when a problem becomes apparent. (Sample guidelines can be found here.)

It is also helpful, at the beginning of the semester, to focus on group processes. Activities and assignments during the first weeks of the course should include opportunities for instructors to get to know each student and for students to get to know one another. Establishing rules for classroom dialogues, building a trusting and open environment, modeling appropriate behavior during dialogues, and giving students the opportunity to practice these behaviors with topics that are not explosive or fearful are important for positive dialogue experiences. If you and your students engage in these behaviors early on, when problems arise, you will be able to address the problem by discussing the rules and appropriate behaviors.

Grouping Students for Learning

There are a variety of reasons for using cooperative groups (to facilitate student learning, to improve interpersonal relationships among students, to foster responsibility for students' own learning and the learning of others, etc.). You might create in-class and/or out-of-class groups (lab groups, homework groups, problem-solving groups, study groups, etc.). Because group composition can have a significant impact on group functioning, you should use a variety of methods to create groups. Such methods include: assigning students to groups (e.g., make heterogeneous groups across certain characteristics such as gender, race, and/or level of achievement in a particular discipline, or by where students live), randomly assigning students (e.g., ask students to draw a piece of paper with a group number from a bag), or allowing students to form their own groups. This latter method should be used sparingly, if possible, as it can consciously or unconsciously be used to create or reinforce social group differences within the class.

In addition to group formation issues, pay attention to the length of time students remain in the same group, particularly if the group is not working together well. It is essential that you address process issues when students work in groups, and some class time should be allocated in the planning of the course to discuss group process issues throughout the semester. It is often helpful for each person in a group to have a specific role (e.g., observer, encourager, summarizer) and everyone should have an opportunity to participate in every role during the semester. You should help students determine a way to provide feedback to one another about group process and dynamics and a way to keep you aware of within-group functioning. Feedback is particularly important for identifying social identity characteristics that might be a source of problems in groups and for figuring out how to address problems satisfactorily. The following guidelines may be useful for addressing group process.

When groups are used, make sure that the same individuals do not always put themselves in the position of leadership. Assigning students to roles (e.g., recorder/notetaker, reporter, moderator) or asking students to rotate roles should reduce the occurrence of this problem.

Be ready to challenge assumptions that groups will either be aided or hindered by having certain kinds of students in their group (e.g., men in math or science classes feeling they have to help the women along; white students working on a project on "rap music" who are eager to have an African American student as part of their group). One way to reduce the likelihood of such assumptions manifesting themselves in group work would be to spend some time informing the class that each individual brings a different combination of strengths and weaknesses into the group work context and that students should not make assumptions about what these might be prior to any interaction with an individual. Group exercises that identify the specific resources that each group member brings can be useful in the early stages of group formation. It is also important to inform students of your availability to discuss group process problems that the groups themselves have been unable to successfully address.

You may need to make an extra effort to reduce the chances that a student who is different from the majority of the class will feel isolated (an African American student in a predominantly white class; a male in a predominantly female class; an openly gay, lesbian, or bisexual student in a class composed predominantly of heterosexuals, etc.). For example, if students are shunning a classmate during small group activities because their classmate is gay and they are homophobic, you (irrespective of your personal perspective on homosexuality) have a responsibility to intervene on behalf of the excluded student. Even when guidelines have been established for participation and responsibilities within groups, problems may arise. It is essential to act quickly when they do. You could begin by reviewing the guidelines for group work. An initial change (if students are forming their own groups) would be to assign individuals to groups and make sure each individual within the group has a role. Another option would be to put students in pairs. It is more difficult to exclude an individual when there are only two participants. If all else fails, it would be important to set up a meeting with the excluded student and together you could generate a variety of actions that could be taken to improve the classroom climate. This would be a show of support to the student. While it is important to solicit student input, you cannot expect the student to have the time or experience to solve the problem. If efforts are made to improve the situation and little change occurs, you might speak with a consultant from CRLT.

Getting to Know the Students

Part of good teaching involves spending some time focusing on building relationships with your students. It is important to some students that you demonstrate caring and genuine concern about them. You may have more positive experiences with students if you invest some time and energy into becoming informed and more aware of issues affecting students of various backgrounds.

One way to get to know your students better early in the semester is to have students write a brief autobiography; it can be as short as two pages. The autobiography can be framed in ways that are relevant to the course content. For example, if you are responsible for math or science courses, you can ask students to share their early experiences (formal and informal) with math and science. They could also be asked to reflect on what their previous experiences with math or science suggest about how they learn best. From this brief paper, you would receive some valuable information about students' attitudes about the content and some of their instructional needs. This kind of assignment could help you to explore, early on, some of the assumptions you might hold about your students and their experiences. It may also help students feel that real interest is being taken in them.

Throughout the term, you can make use of office hours, written assignments, and class discussion to further develop your knowledge about and connections to students. Specific suggestions have already been made in previous sections of this chapter.

Decisions, Comments, & Behaviors During the Teaching Process

If you are responsible for teaching sections of a course, it is essential to understand that even when you have limited input into course content, you have much control over how that content gets taught. Teaching is a complex activity in which there are multiple levels of interaction among students and between GSIs and students. Students all bring very different backgrounds, knowledge, and learning styles to a particular course. There are multiple interpretations of content constructed by individual students during the learning process. Also, some students construct different images of their instructors which are counter to how you might see yourself. Because of the complexity and unpredictability of teaching, you should carefully plan your course sessions and always be prepared for the unexpected to occur. The following points address many of the issues that may arise during the teaching process.

Working with Course Content

Examine course content for inaccurate information and the absence of relevant perspectives. Prepare for each class session by reading upcoming assignments in order to identify omissions, misleading interpretations, and intentional or inadvertent expressions of personal opinion by the author. You may then alert students to problems with the text and encourage students to read critically themselves. For example, a section on employment discrimination in an Economics text states that blatant racial or gender discrimination is vanishing today. Since this is a statement about which there is current disagreement, students might be prompted to consider and discuss their own degree of agreement with this statement.

Be careful about the comments made during class lectures, discussions, recitation sessions, etc. Be aware of the fact that comments that are not fully explained may inadvertently invoke stereotypes or promote inaccurate conclusions. Similarly, skewed examples of religious, historical, or other events have the potential to lead students to believe that inaccuracies are truths.

Student Critiques of Course Content

Inclusive Strategies for the Virtual Classroom

Create a classroom climate that encourages and expects questions about and critiques of course content. Such a climate will help to create a norm of critical thinking that will facilitate the learning process for all students. As students share their critiques with the class, other students will benefit by being exposed to different interpretations, perspectives, and concerns regarding course material. This climate can also provide an opportunity for students to add to the course content by correcting inaccuracies or misrepresentations related to the history or experience of their own groups.

Make decisions about when to devote unanticipated time to class discussions to deal with issues raised by students that pertain to content or process. These issues, which may deal with the history or culture of a group with which you are unfamiliar, are an equally important part of the course content. It is best to be honest about your lack of knowledge, acknowledge the students' point, and make efforts to secure information about the students' point to share with the class in a future session. It is also important to emphasize that everyone can be a teacher and that instructors and students can learn from one another. You can also ask students to send you e-mail messages, chat with you during office hours, or drop notes in you mailbox as concerns about course content arise. You should make every effort to address these issues or explain to students why they will not be addressed.

Be open to students' reactions to course material, even when you feel uncomfortable with the manner in which they are expressed. Be prepared for students to publicly challenge inaccurate information about particular groups that appears in class readings, films, etc. Students may react strongly upon hearing what they perceive to be inaccurate and negative information about their group. You may find yourself teaching courses that have the reputation (from the students' perspective) of being full of inaccurate or misleading content. Students can often feel unduly burdened when they are in a position as teacher rather than learner. Students may resent having to "pick up the slack" in classes where instructors and their peers lack knowledge about the group with which the particular students are affiliated. When students are of the opinion that the information being given in the course is biased against their group, they may feel that they are also missing valuable learning opportunities. Creating a positive learning experience for these students can be challenging. In this situation, it is most important to be open to the perspectives these students share. Giving serious consideration to students' views that are in the "minority" will encourage students to respond honestly about issues while also encouraging students to think more broadly about issues. This does not, however, mean that you have to agree with the students' views or feel that the students' views are above critique.

Give serious consideration to students' requests for alternative materials when materials currently used inaccurately represent aspects of students' social identity groups or cultures. Changes should be made when justified. If you receive criticisms about materials, you should make clear to students that the criticism can be accompanied by specific recommendations of alternative materials.

Responding to Student Identities

Invite all students to contribute to class discussion, even if you assume that the discussion is more relevant to some students than others. Students (irrespective of background) do not like being forced to serve as the spokesperson for their group. Students also do not appreciate being expected to know everything about issues relating to their group or the assumption that all students from their group feel the same way about an issue.

Be sensitive to the experiences of visibly underrepresented students in your class. Students with identities that are underrepresented and visible or known may face certain challenges that unfairly compromise their learning environment. For example, students may not be allowed to do assignments on certain topics because of the instructor's assumption about the students' biases. In one course, women wearing Islamic head scarves were readily identified as Muslim and not allowed to write a paper on Islam; it was more difficult to readily identify students as Christian from their appearance, so they were not prevented from writing papers on Christianity. Students from underrepresented groups may also feel a self-imposed pressure always to portray themselves in a good light so they do not reinforce stereotypes about their group. Whereas "majority students" can slack off from time to time when working within groups, occasionally show up late to class, or be absent without peers attributing their behavior to membership in a particular group, students from underrepresented groups often sense that their behavior is interpreted as a reflection on their group. Although there may be little you can do to relieve this self-imposed pressure on the part of some students, you can be thoughtful about your interactions with these students and make an effort not to publicly discuss students' performance or behavior.

Inequities in the Classroom

Be aware of gender dynamics in classroom discussions. Even when women are in the majority, men may sometimes consciously or unconsciously dominate class discussions or interrupt women.

Monitor the occurrence of this behavior and encourage women to speak up at the same time they discourage men from dominating the discussion.

Be careful not to respond to comments in ways that students might interpret as dismissals. You should give sufficient attention to (a) students' comments that differ from the majority of students' views or your own views, (b) students' views that are based on experiential knowledge, and (c) women's views in predominately male classes or traditionally male fields. Be aware of differential feedback given to students who differ on some aspect of their social identity (gender, ethnicity, disability, sexual orientation, etc.). For example, you should attend to whether you speak down to women or "brush off" their questions, yet give men responses that are informative and detailed.

Conflict in the Classroom

Respond to classroom conflict in a manner that helps students become aware of the "learning moment" this conflict provides. Heated discussions need to be facilitated in a manner that does not result in hostility among class members and a sustained sense of bad feeling in the room. You can avoid these outcomes by encouraging students to tie their feelings and conflicts to the course material and by looking for underlying meanings and principles that might get buried in the process of class conflict. Students appreciate tensions between groups in the class being recognized and effectively addressed.

Recognize student fears and concerns about conflict. Students enter a class with different levels of experience and comfort with conflict. It is important to normalize the experience of conflict in the classroom, particularly in classes that focus on controversial topics. This can be accomplished through explicit discussion of student experiences with conflict and the use of structured discussion exercises.

Maintain the role of facilitator. One of the challenges of teaching is maintaining the role of instructor under a variety of conditions. For example, you can get caught up in expressing your own perspective in heated discussions or can become overly silent in discussions that go beyond your own knowledge base or experience. While these responses are understandable, such role abdication can create chaos in the classroom or force students to fill in the abdicated facilitator role. In order to avoid this outcome, you should examine your typical responses to conflict. It can also be useful to find ways that you may admit your limits with respect to content areas while maintaining responsibility for the group process.

Be Virtually Inclusive: Do's and Don't For Educators

Schools are rapidly shifting to online learning, at least for now. So that means you are likely to begin the school year much differently than ever before. It's now time to embrace the season we are in and adapt to new teaching methods. Effective teachers are resilient and therefore capable of creating sustainable online classrooms when they are all in. Unfortunately, there's a good chance that online classrooms may never feel the same as live instruction, but we can do our very best to make our virtual classes come to life. While planning out your lessons it's important to consider how you will ensure that your classroom is inclusive and accessible for all learners. While you may be teaching from behind a screen this year, don't let the screen box in your thinking! Students need to feel a sense of belonging, and they also need to be able to access course materials. What principles of inclusive/ accessible teaching are you drawing upon that will help students feel accepted this year? How will you support them in achieving learning goals while you are teaching them online? Empathy and resilience on the part of both students and instructors will be of the essence. To help guide you toward full inclusion and accessibility with your virtual classroom this week's blog will give you do's, don'ts, and other simple ways to modify your virtual classroom design to create space that will accommodate learners and inspire them to do their best work.

Why is an inclusive learning environment important?

Encouraging and continuing inclusive learning environments is important to allow all students to be able to fully participate, engage, and learn. The online learning environment obliges educators to think creatively about how to achieve this goal. To assist you as you are designing your online virtual space and holding your first online classes, the following suggestions, guidance, and resource information can be used to help you develop an inclusive learning environment in your virtual classroom.

A welcoming and inclusive class culture is one that recognizes the diversity and encourages student engagement and belonging. These elements are critical for students' learning and can be encouraged by creating a social presence and by building and promoting connections among and between students and teachers. Furthermore, it is important to communicate your expectations for interactions and student engagement to model appropriate and thoughtful student interactions and communication. The information presented below is aimed at helping provide you with some general guidelines for building an inclusive virtual classroom environment.

General guidance on building online classrooms that support inclusive learning: Dos and Don'ts

A modified list based on guidance from Northwestern:

Do - Create shared rules and expectations.

Don't - Create rules and expectations without buy-in from students.

When you create shared rules and expectations it can help avoid miscommunication, disrespectful language, and hurt feelings, and can foster a constructive exchange of perspectives, opinions, approaches, and viewpoints.

Do - Recognize challenging circumstances

Don't - Ignore or assume challenging circumstances

Students and parents may have a range of emotions related to the current COVID-19 crisis, economic struggles, and the global response to social injustices occurring.

Do - Build a social presence

Don't - make yourself scarce and unavailable to your students

To build your social presence, use icebreaker activities at the beginning and throughout your class. However, keep in mind that you don't pose questions that will require students to disclose potentially sensitive information about themselves. To further promote your social presence, introduce yourself to your students, and let them know something about who you are. Another thing that will help build your presence is to check in with your students often via email or phone call. Try check-ins with students via email and establish online office hours. Consider holding required one-on-one meetings for your students to get individualized attention. For some additional help watch this video "Translating In-Person Teaching Online," from the Searle Center for Advancing Learning and Teaching. This short video will teach you how to navigate Zoom and implement whiteboards, annotations, breakouts, and other techniques to help you create community among your students, build social presence, and ease students' discomfort.

Do -Promote equitable participation in your class by providing students multiple ways to participate.

Don't - use just one way to get your students involved in your class.

Check out this guide from the University of Michigan on Best Practices for incorporating active learning in your class.

Do - Monitor Student interactions

Don't - Assume that students are interacting according to the norms you set.

Be intentional about consistently reviewing your class norms and the expectations for communicating respectfully with others.

Cultural Inclusiveness Matters!

Read this list of do's and don'ts for virtual classroom cultural inclusiveness courtesy of Tanisha Forman: To see 5 practices you can incorporate into your virtual classroom.

Do Represent - Regardless of the demographics of your classroom, students need to see themselves and others represented in the classroom. Review your books, project units, math problems, quotes, and other instructional materials and double-check that names and visual images represent students from different backgrounds.

DON'T use stereotypes to guide decisions. All Black American students aren't fans of Hip Hop. Additionally, if you have a class with one person of color, don't call on them to read the problem/story with a character you perceive to be similar, or look to them as the voice of an entire group of people.

Do Affirm - Get to know students and their backgrounds. Affirm them by learning how they learn best, what makes them tick, what keeps them engaged, and how to best communicate with them. For example, in some cultures, looking people in the eyes can be considered disrespectful.

DON'T force students into practices that don't work for them, or take a "one size fits all" approach. Remember that fair is not equal.

Do Keep High Expectations - All students regardless of their backgrounds deserve to be held to highest expectations. Teachers should be explicit with their expectations so that students are clear on what to do to be successful in the class. Celebrate these expectations in a manner that communicates your commitment to students and their learning trajectory.

DON'T make excuses for students or base high expectations based solely on the normative culture.

Do Address Breaches - When something happens that aims at someone's identity, it must be addressed. Not addressing it will have an impact on your culture and how students feel in your classroom. Children may say something to you, or their offensive peers, and as the leader of the classroom, teachers have a responsibility to address it. We aren't perfect, but we are adults. Not sure how to respond? Consider the following:

Take a moment to recognize what happened

Journal activity

Ask the person(s) impacted what will help

Have a peer conference

Discuss it in a morning meeting

Use an "Anonymous Jar" to have students write out their thoughts/feelings and discuss

DON'T - Make light of serious situations, or ignore them. Remember, not saying something, says something!

Do maintain relationships with key stakeholders - It's not always easy, but continuously make an effort to get to know the people who matter the most to students. There are some natural moments that we have (parent/teacher conferences, report card discussions, ect.), but teachers should have touchpoints in between those moments. Not always easy, but proves to students that you care about them. Additionally, consider getting to know how guardians like to receive their communication (text, email, call). The tough part is restoring relationships with guardians that might not have gotten off on the right foot, or that have taken a turn in the wrong direction.

DON'T - only contact parents/guardians when there's an issue, or as the "main consequence" for students.

Students with disabilities need to feel included and virtual classes must be accessible for them to thrive!

For most educators teaching students online is something you've never had to do until now. In preparation for a significant change, the majority of teachers spent most of their time in the past months creating an online classroom and a welcoming virtual space to call home for their classroom this year. Trying to figure out how this new system of teaching will work may have had teachers caught up on the design to make sure it looked inviting, and interesting for students. Many teachers could have unintentionally found themselves overwhelmed with how they will support their students with various disabilities. In the past with in-person classroom instruction, inclusion and accessibility may have had its challenges but by making the transition to virtual classrooms, these challenges may have become greater. Traditionally students with disabilities were always taught in an in-person setting, yet some research from various sources suggests that students with disabilities learn quite well online if they have the right set up, design, and resources to support their learning style. However, because distance learning has not been widely instituted as it has been today there is yet to be a ton of research on how to ensure that your virtual classroom is inclusive and accessible for all students.

Inclusive Strategies for the Virtual Classroom

But what does "accessible" mean in a virtual setting?

According to the Office of Civil Rights, "accessible" means that "a person with a disability is allowed to acquire the same information, engage in the same interactions, and enjoy the same services as a person without a disability in an equally effective and integrated manner, with substantially equivalent ease of use. The person with a disability must be able to obtain the information as fully, equally, and independently as a person without a disability."

Why is ensuring accessibility in your virtual classroom important?

Students with learning disabilities may have unknown difficulties with virtual online learning environments and classrooms that are predominantly text-based or lecture-based. Given these challenges, it is still important for teachers to be able to ensure that all students have resources and adaptive equipment that will allow students with disabilities to participate regardless of the disability they may have. Fortunately, there are many software products and assistive aids designed to assist students and others with disabilities to be able to access the necessary tools and equipment to participate in virtual settings. Software products that read text aloud such as ReadPlease and other text to speech programs are just one example of tools and resources available to help students and help educators to teach students. Additionally, textbooks can be loaded into wireless reading devices that can make reading easier by allowing students to increase the font size and use it with black letters on a white background.

Overall, the law's for persons and students with disabilities still apply, therefore we must all work together to figure out best practices to ensure students with disabilities can learn without in a virtual setting. In our quest to provide you with information on best practices we came across a project in the UK. A group of colleagues got together a few years ago to design a series of posters that project dos and don'ts of designing for accessibility to be used as general guidelines and best design practices for making services accessible in government in the UK. Many of these design practices may also be useful to educators who are transitioning their classrooms from in-person to virtual. At the end of the day, students need to be able to access the information you are presenting or requesting them to participate in during your online class. To provide you with some accessibility tips check out the list of do's and don'ts below provided by Karwai Pun and her team of designers.

Do's and Don'ts for being inclusive with accessibility online

Check Karwai Pun's general list of do's and don'ts to see if any of these do's can be adopted and incorporated into your online virtual classroom practices. (Click the title to view the illustration!)

Designing for users on the autistic spectrum.

Do

- use simple colors
- write in plain English
- use simple sentences and bullets
- make buttons descriptive - for example, Attach files here
- build simple and consistent layouts

Don't

- use bright contrasting colors
- use figures of speech and idioms
- create a wall of text

- make buttons vague and unpredictable - for example, "Click here"
- build complex and cluttered layouts

Designing for users of screen readers

Do

- describe images and provide transcripts for video
- follow a linear, logical layout
- structure content using HTML5
- build for keyboard use only
- write descriptive links and heading - for example, Contact me

Don't

- only show information in an image or video
- spread content all over a page
- rely on text size and placement for structure
- force mouse or screen use
- write uninformative links and heading - for example, "Click here"

Designing for users with low vision

Do

- use good contrasts and a readable font size

- use a combination of color, shapes, and text
- follow a linear, logical layout -and ensure text flows and is visible when text is magnified to 200%
- put buttons and notifications in context

Don't

- use low color contrasts and small font size
- bury information in downloads
- only use color to convey meaning
- spread content all over a page -and force the user to scroll horizontally when text is magnified to 200%
- separate actions from their context

Designing for users with physical or motor disabilities

Do

- make large clickable actions
- give form fields space
- design for keyboard or speech only use
- design with mobile and touch screen in mind

provide shortcuts

Don't

- demand precision
- bunch interactions together
- make dynamic content that requires a lot of mouse movement

- have short timeout windows
- tire users with lots of typing and scrolling

Designing for users who are deaf or hard of hearing

Do

- Write in plain English
- Use subtitles or provide transcripts for video
- Use a linear, logical layout
- Break up content with subheadings, images, and videos
- Let students ask for their preferred communication support

Don't

- Use complicated words or figures of speech
- Put content in audio or video only
- Make complex layouts and menus
- Make users read long blocks of content
- Don't make telephone the only means of contact for students

Inclusive Strategies for the Virtual Classroom

Designing for users with dyslexia.

Do

- Use images and diagrams to support text
- Align text to the left and keep a consistent layout
- Consider producing materials in other formats (for example, audio and video)
- Keep content short, clear and simple
- Let users change the contrast between background and text

Don't

- Use large blocks of heavy text
- Underline words, use italics or write capitals

- Force students to remember things from previous pages - give reminders and prompts
- Rely on accurate spelling - use autocorrect or provide suggestions
- Put too much information in one place

Additional Programs/Resources

For some additional tips and guidance visit 20-tips-teaching-accessible-online-course by Burgstahler, Sheryl, Ph.D. from the University at Washington who taught the very first online learning course at the University of Washington in 1995. Her co-instructor was Dr. Norm Coombs, who was, at the time, a professor at the Rochester Institute of Technology. Together they designed the course to be accessible to anyone, including students who were blind, deaf or had physical disabilities. Dr. Burgstahler claims that Norm himself was blind. He used a screen-reader and speech synthesizer to read text presented on the screen. They employed the latest technology of the time such as; email, discussion list, Gopher, file transfer protocol, and telnet (The World Wide Web did not exist in1995!). All online materials were in a text-based format, and videos, which were mailed to the students, were presented in VHS format with captions and audio description. When asked if any of their students in this course had disabilities, they were proud to say that they did not know. No one needed to disclose a disability because all of the course materials and teaching methods were designed to be accessible to everyone. Today however technology is much more advanced so naturally there are a plethora of methods and ways you can use to ensure your virtual classroom is accessible to all students.

If you found this information interesting or useful, let us know by submitting your feedback! We would love to hear what you have to say about the topics that we share and what you would like to hear more.

Quick Ways to Be More Inclusive in a Virtual Classroom

How do you create online or hybrid courses with an ethos of inclusion and equity embedded throughout?

If you're teaching this fall, you're probably trying to figure out how your courses will be affected by the dual reverberations of Covid-19 and Black Lives Matter. Being prepared for an uncertain semester means both improving your remote-teaching skills and finding ways to make your classroom more inclusive.

The two aims overlap, given that online teaching will figure heavily in the coming semester. This month's column turns to inclusive teaching in a virtual classroom.

The ethos of an equitable and inclusive classroom is simple: "Everybody gets to learn. No one has to out themselves. All are welcome. All are supported by the very design of this class." The hard part: How do you create online or hybrid courses with that ethos embedded throughout? Two frameworks in your teaching toolkit — Universal Design for Learning and culturally responsive pedagogy — create a powerful way forward. Let's look at each in turn.

Universal Design for Learning. UDL takes research on how people learn and applies it to course design and teaching. A good way to think about this is to consider the concept of "universal design" in architecture. Picture a ramp alongside a set of stairs; both lead up to a building entrance. The ramp was constructed to help wheelchair users get where they want to go — that is, into the building. But the ramp benefits others, too: people using walkers, strollers, luggage on wheels, or cargo dollies. The ramp wasn't originally conceived for them but once it's in place, they benefit from it, too.

UDL applies that idea to the classroom. It's about offering choices — akin to the stairs or the ramp — to support learning and get students where they want to go. With UDL, you can plan your course from the outset in ways that, while they lower barriers to learning for students with certain needs, benefit all students. Specifically, this approach flips the idea of needing to provide an accommodation in class for a student with disabilities — something that risks stigmatizing the student and imposes extra work on a faculty member. Instead of rushing to adapt to a last-minute accommodation for a particular student, UDL helps you design "ramps" as part of your course, so they're already in place for anyone who needs (or wants) to take advantage of them.

A classic example of UDL for an online course is providing captions for or transcripts of videos. Prerecorded videos (as I've noted before) are a great way to communicate and build connections with online students. Besides being easy to create, videos are a powerful means of explaining complicated concepts and are more efficient than Zoom teaching

You can reuse your videos in future semesters, too, if you make the content evergreen.

Universal Design for Learning

	Recognition learning	Strategic learning	Affective learning
3 primary networks			
3 principles of UDL	Representation	Action & expression	Engagement
3 sets of UDL guidelines	Flexible ways to present **what** we teach and learn.	Flexible options for **how** we learn and express what we know.	Flexible options for generating and sustaining motivation, the **why** of learning.

But videos need captions in order to be of use to students with hearing loss. Instead of letting that extra step — and extra work — stop you from creating videos, think of it as a way to lower barriers for everyone in your class. Many students prefer to read along while they watch an instructional video; it helps them absorb and process information. A text transcript is a good alternative to captions (or you can offer both). Some students like to print out transcripts, take notes on them, and then use them to study for a quiz. The point again: By offering this option to help students with hearing loss, you aid all students.

Ready to use UDL in designing your online courses for the fall? There are loads of options, but here are some simple, practical ideas to get you started:

- Provide the same course content in two different formats. I just mentioned a good example of this — videos with captions — but there are many other ways to do it. Give students a piece of text, and offer the same content in a visual format such as a chart or infographic. Or, when you ask students to read a chapter of the textbook, make an audio file of you reading it, so students can "read" it on the go or to absorb new ideas in a way that works best for them.
- Allow two options for how students can complete an assignment. For example, permit them to submit a weekly reflection on their learning either in writing or by smartphone video. Some students process information and express their ideas better in speech than in writing.
- Offer students a choice in completing a final project. Will a

research paper or a video presentation enable students to achieve the learning goals and show what they know? Let them decide which one they prefer to create.

Does all of this sound like a lot of work for faculty members? It doesn't have to be. Nor does it have to cost a lot of time or money. Thomas J. Tobin, a distance-learning guru at the University of Wisconsin at Madison, advocates a "plus-one" approach to UDL: Simply add one option to help your students engage with the content in ways they prefer.

Culturally Responsive Pedagogy. An equally important consideration for the fall is how you will support culturally diverse learners in your online courses. Especially at this moment in American history, you must think critically about how to help Black, Latinx, and other students in historically underrepresented groups succeed in your online (or in-person) courses.

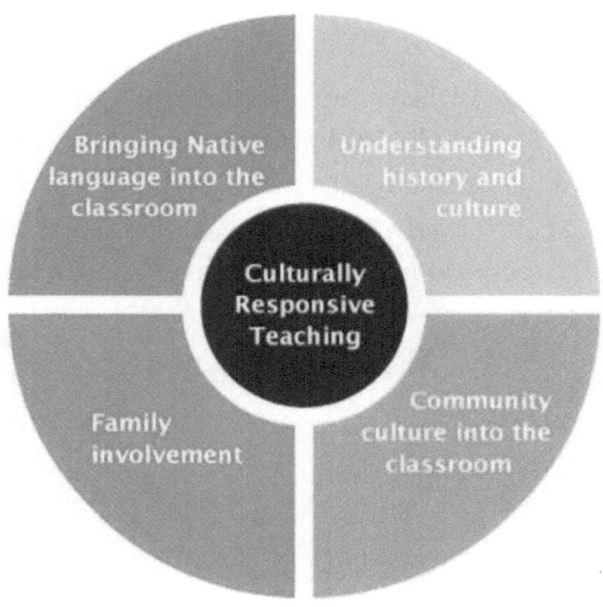

Courtney Plotts is a researcher and educator who specializes in supporting culturally diverse students in online classes. Her recent interview on the Teaching in Higher Ed podcast is a good place to start. There and elsewhere, she argues that online classes function in very transactional and Eurocentric ways. Students who do best in online courses, she says, are self-directed learners, have been shaped by cultures that value individual well-being, or both. What about students from cultures that value community over individual success? What about students who, for a variety of good reasons, don't possess a strong self-identity, or who feel uncertain or worried about asking the instructor for help?

This is a complicated, sensitive subject. But again, there are simple, practical things you can do to be more equitable and inclusive in your online teaching. Here are a few of Plotts's suggestions:

- Lead an exercise asking students to help set classroom values. Create a Padlet (an online visual Post-it board with limitless uses in teaching), and ask students to post words and images that represent what's important to them in a classroom. Students might come up with things like respecting all perspectives, creating and maintaining a safe space for all, engaging in civil discourse, using person-centered language, etc. You can refine their ideas into a list or leave them gloriously unstructured on Padlet. Revisit these co-constructed values throughout the term, asking how well the class is doing in upholding them. You can try an anonymous survey or poll, a classwide discussion, or both, for different purposes.
- "Which picture best describes how you're feeling?" Here's a quick exercise (another good use of Padlet) to help you gauge how students of different backgrounds feel about your online

course. Provide a variety of images — a serene landscape, a feisty cat, a race car, a stormy sea cliff, a mournful hound dog — and ask students to write or record themselves talking about which one best represents how they feel, whether about online learning, about the fall semester, about the subject matter, or about anything else you want to know about. Best suited for a small class, this activity shows students that you care about them as people and are not fixated on just their meeting class deadlines. Follow up by emailing those students who selected images that conveyed anxiety or other negative emotions, and periodically check in with them throughout the semester.

- Remind them to reach out to you for help. Be aware, Plotts says, that students from some cultural backgrounds may hesitate to ask an instructor for assistance. The same goes for introverted students. In remote teaching, you can use announcements, short recorded videos, and email messages to encourage students to contact you, even if it's outside their comfort zone. Repeat that message frequently enough for them to believe you mean it. Use a warm and encouraging tone. Respond quickly to their emails and questions. All of that will encourage students to take you up on your offer.

Be patient with yourself as you try these new approaches. Both UDL and culturally responsive pedagogy can feel overwhelming. So do just one new thing this fall. Add another in the spring, or improve upon your approach from the fall. We say we support our students. We say we want all of them to learn and succeed. Let's show them we mean it by working to lower barriers in our course design.

Inclusive online teaching: 6 tips for the virtual classroom

Whether you are doing synchronous or asynchronous online instruction, distance learning can feel impersonal and inaccessible. But there are strategies for inclusive online teaching to help students feel a sense of connection and inclusion.

Earlier this year when governments locked down amidst the COVID-19 pandemic, teachers around the region rushed to create sustainable virtual spaces as learning abruptly went online.

While Zoom, Google Meet, and Microsoft Teams won't feel the same as classroom face to face instruction, many of us are faced with either continued home-based learning or a blend of in-person and e-Learning as social distancing measures continue.

Once you have your students' mobile device management for education in place, here are 6 ways we can create virtual classrooms that engage and inspire all learners.

Show that you care

A small gesture goes a long way. Start your class with a greeting and let the students see your smile. Virtual learning can still be awkward for many students. The human touch makes students feel welcome when coming to your class.

Inclusive online teaching shows that you care. Before jumping into the lesson of the day, ask them, "How are you feeling today?" E-Learning for kids can affect mental wellbeing.

If a student replies to you directly on the chat function, send them a private message to show you are listening.

Set Operational Procedures

You are in control of the virtual learning space. Mobile device management for education is paramount. Anticipate and prevent distractions in the virtual classroom by setting clear rules and expectations and that includes mobile device management. Best practices are to communicate your expectations at the start of each lesson, each day.

Be concise and highlight behaviors that directly affect everyone's virtual learning experience, such as "Use the chat function to type questions" or "Mute your microphone during presentations."

If your students intentionally break your rules so that it interrupts the virtual learning experience, remove them from the virtual learning environment, and contact their parents to check that everyone is clear on the expectations.

Inclusive Strategies for the Virtual Classroom

What's the plan?

A virtual classroom can be a challenge in education structure and organization. Set the day's agenda by sharing a learning target so that everyone knows what to expect from the lesson. As attention tends to be shorter in virtual learning spaces, be mindful of how long you can hold the attention of your group, providing breaks as necessary.

As with in-person learning, a virtual classroom with inclusive online teaching has a predictable structure that makes students feel more at ease with their learning.

Try different engagement techniques

You may or may not have the latest educational technology. Regardless of how simple or feature-rich your learning platform or video conferencing is, see what's possible. There are creative ways to use it to engage your students.

- Students can show their thinking by sharing their screen
- Students can offer feedback to a classmate's work over chat
- Have students read out loud to each other
- Praise good work by sharing your screen

Hold Virtual Office Hours

As with face to face classroom learning, some students need more help. Set your virtual office hours and have your door open for someone looking for some extra time with their teacher.

Incentivize your virtual office hours. One way is by issuing a weekly raffle ticket to encourage your students to seek help when they need it. At the end of the week, pick a winner!

Reach out and support families

Students and their families may be facing multiple challenges at this time. This could be a time of financial hardship for many. Is your student at home alone and looking after a younger sibling as the parents are working?

Do they have the proper devices and internet access to access e-learning? Does your learner have a quiet space where they can go to focus on their work?

Reach out and check in with your families at least once a week. Show that you care: see what their struggles are and update them on their student's progress.

Some of your students may need more frequent check-ins at first so make time every day to reach out. Your efforts will be invaluable.

It's possible that as the teacher you may be providing tech support to get parents and students and students online. Be patient and prepared to answer any technical questions about your learning platform. To make it easier, create a reference sheet or short explainer video.

The human touch goes a long way. Have empathy and reach out from a place of support and communicate positively: What can I do to support him? Do you have everything you need for virtual and online learning?"

www.ingramcontent.com/pod-product-compliance
Lightning Source LLC
Chambersburg PA
CBHW030502220526
45464CB00006B/2625